AF413529

CURSIVE WRITING

Book for 3rd Graders

Bible Story Edition

Children's Reading and Writing Books

Let's Begin Writing!

THE
CREATION

In the beginning
there was no earth
or sky or sea or
animals. And then
God spoke in the
darkness. "Let

there be light!" And

right away there

was light, scattering
the darkness and
showing the infinite
space. "That's
good!" said God.
"From now on,

when it's dark it
will be 'night' and
when it's light, it
will be day."

The evening came

and the night passed

and then the light

returned. That was

the first day.

On the second

day, God made
the earth and over
it He carefully
hung a vast blue
sky. He stood back
and admired His

creation. "That's

good too!" said

God and the second

day was over.

The next morning

God looked around
and thought,
"The earth needs
to be a bit more
organized." So, He
put all the water

in one place and

all the dry land in

another. When He
had finished that,
God made plants
to cover the land.
Dandelions and
daffodils appeared.

All sorts of trees
and grasses began to
grow. "It's looking
great," said God
and that was the
end of the third day.

On the fourth day,

God looked around

and thought, "The

daylight still needs a

bit more work and

the night is just too

dark." So, He made

the sun to light the
sky during the day
and the moon and
stars to add a bit
of sparkle to the
night. He hung

them in the sky and
stepped back to look
at his work. "This is
coming along very
well," said God.

The next day, God turned his attention to the water he had collected in the oceans. "I want these waters teeming

with life!" As soon
as He said it, it
was so. In no time,
there were millions
of small fish darting
through the shallow

water and huge
fish swimming in
the ocean. God
made birds, too. He
sent them soaring
through the air.

"Ahh, that IS
good!" said God.
The dusk fell over
the water and the
sky grew dark and
that was the end of

the fifth day.

On the sixth day,
God added creatures
to the land. He
made lions and
tigers and bears. He
made rabbits and

sheep and cows. He
added everything
from ants to zebras
to the land. But He
still felt something
was missing.

So God added

Mankind to enjoy

and take care of all
that He had created.
God looked around
and was happy with
all He had made.

After six days, the
whole universe was
completed. On the
seventh day God
had a nice long rest
and enjoyed looking

at all He had made.

THE STORY OF
ADAM & EVE

God took some clay
from the ground

and made the shape

of a man. Then He

breathed gently into

the shape. The man's

eye's opened and he

began to live. God

called him Adam.

The Lord made a
beautiful garden for
him to live in. The
garden, called Eden,

was full of many

wonderful things.

God had made the

man in His image

to keep Him

company and look
after the world.

God brought all the
animals to Adam
one at a time to be

given their names.

But God felt sorry

for Adam. "None of

these animals is

really like him."

thought God. "he
needs someone to
share his life.
Someone who cares
for him and who he
can care for."

That night, God
took a rib from
Adam's side and
made a woman.
When Adam awoke
the following

morning, he found
a wife, Eve, lying
asleep beside him.
Adam was so
happy. He took her
hand and she woke

up.

God told the man

and woman that it

was their job to take

care of their new

home. God blessed
them, saying, "All
this is for you. But
never touch the tree
in the middle of
the Garden. That

tree gives knowledge

of good and evil.

The day you eat its

fruit, you will die."

One day, Adam and

Eve were gathering
berries for dinner
when she heard a
voice behind her.
"Has God told you

that you can eat
the fruit from all
the trees?" the voice
asked softly. Eve
turned around to see
a snake talking to

hea.

" God has told us

we can eat all the

fruit except for what

grows on the Tree

of the Knowledge of

Good and Evil,"

Eve told the serpent.

"Oh come now,

that's silly! I

hardly think such a

lovely fruit would do

you any harm," the

serpent lied. "God

knows that if you

eat from The Tree

of the Knowledge of

Good and Evil

you'll become just

like God, and will

be able to decide for

yourself what is

right and what is

wrong."

The woman looked
at the fruit and
thought how tasty it
looked. She thought

how wonderful it
would be to be as
wise and powerful
as God. She believed
the serpent's lie and
ate the fruit and

also gave some to

Adam, who was

with her, and he

took a bite as well.
She felt a strange
feeling in the pit
of her stomach.
Suddenly she
realized that she was

feeling guilty — she
had disobeyed God
and knew she'd done
something wrong.

Adam and Eve

heard God calling
them. Without
thinking, they dived
into the bushes, but
God knew where
they were. When

God asked them if
they had eaten
from The Tree of
the Knowledge of
Good and Evil that
He had told them

not to touch, they
blamed each other
for their sins.

God was sad that
Adam and Eve

had disobeyed Him.

He told them that

they had to leave

the Garden of

Eden. "From now

on you'll have to

scratch a living

from the soil. You'll

need to make clothes
and grow food.
Nothing will come
easily — not even
childbirth. And one
day, you will die."

Visit

BABY PROFESSOR
EDUCATION KIDS

www.BabyProfessorBooks.com
to download Free Baby Professor eBooks
and view our catalog of new and exciting
Children's Books